Help with Homework

Math

Especially suitable for grades K-2

BACKPACKBOOKS

○

NEW YORK

Connect the dots

Starting with number 1, connect the dots to complete the picture.

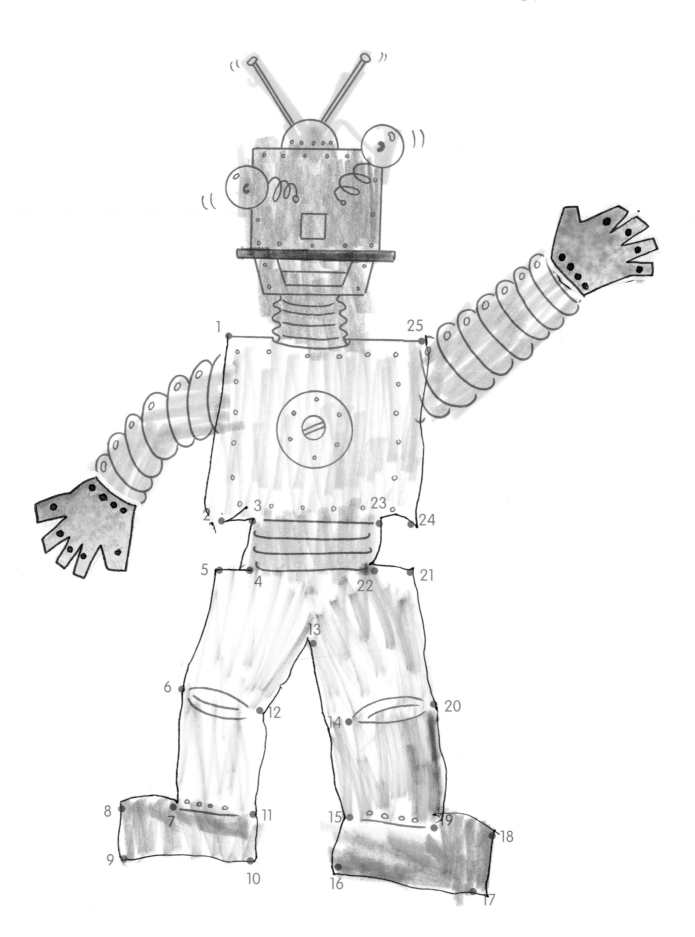

Color by shapes

Follow the code to color the picture.
Choose your own colors where there are no code symbols.

▲ dark green

⬛ brown

◻ light green

Shortest and tallest

Who do you think is the shortest?

Which do you think is the tallest?

Halves

Find the stickers and put them in place. Draw lines from top to bottom or across to divide the objects in half. Color each half in a different color.

Quarters

Find the stickers and put them in place. Draw lines to divide each object into quarters.
Color the quarters in different colors.

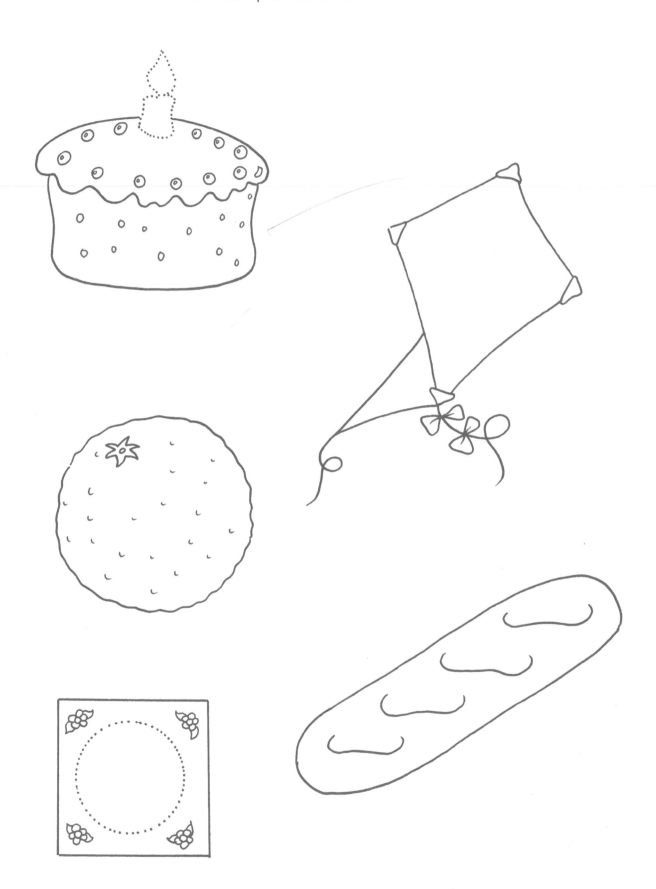

Groups

Find the stickers and put them in place.
Draw a circle around each group of 3 bees. How many groups are there?

Count and add

Find the stickers and put them in place. Count the spots on the butterflies' wings.
Add them up and write the total on the sunflower.

Shapes

How many long, round, oval, and wavy balloons can you see in the picture?
Write the answers in the boxes.

Most and fewest

Count the carrots that each rabbit has.
Which rabbit has the most? Color the carrots orange.
Which rabbit has the fewest? Color these carrots yellow.

Adding

Each mouse has 3 pieces of cheese.
Draw more pieces to add up to the total number in each box.

Number maze

Follow the numbers from 1 to 20 to help the pirate find the treasure chest.

Add and draw

Draw more goldfish so that each pair of aquariums has the same number of fish.

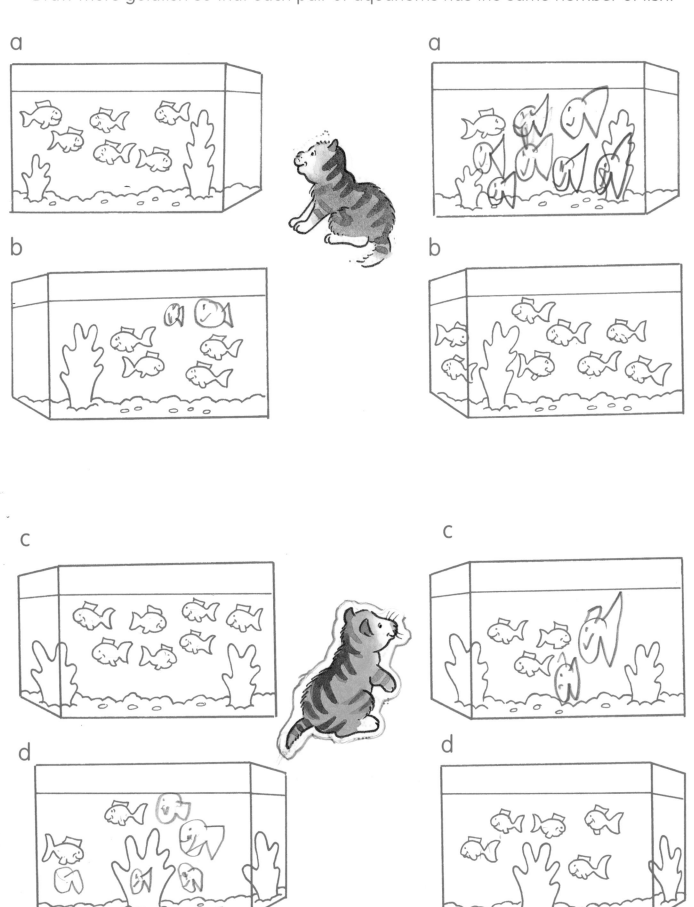

Squirrel subtraction

Find the stickers and put them in place. Do the subtraction and draw a line to connect each answer to the correct group of squirrels.

$$20 - 16 = \qquad 30 - 22 =$$

$$15 - 13 = \qquad 12 - 7 = 9$$

Shapes

Counting each shape once, how many shapes can you see inside each of these kites?
Write the answers in the boxes. Do not count the kite tails or the boxes!

Adding

Do the addition and write the answers in the boxes.

$1 + 2 =$ 3

$6 + 5 =$ 11

$8 + 1 =$ 9

$3 + 3 =$ 6

$4 + 8 =$ 12

$2 + 10 =$ 12

$3 + 5 =$ 8

$9 + 3 =$ 12

$6 + 8 =$ 14

$10 + 10 =$ 20

$4 + 4 =$ 8

$2 + 12 =$ 14

$8 + 8 =$ 16

$9 + 9 =$ 18

$10 + 11 =$ 21

A+

Count and add

Count how many markings each cow has. Write the answers in the boxes.
Add them together to find the total, and write the total in the box.

Total

Matching answers

Find the stickers and put them in place. Do the math on the shorts and T-shirts.
Look for the answers on the children. Draw a line to connect the problem to the answer.

5 + 5 = [8]

14 + 2 = [ ]

15 − 6 = [10]

16

10

Taking away

Do the subtraction and write the answers in the boxes.

$5 - 3 = \boxed{2}$

$6 - 2 = \boxed{4}$

$12 - 6 = \boxed{6}$

$7 - 6 = \boxed{1}$

$3 - 2 = \boxed{1}$

$8 - 5 = \boxed{3}$

$9 - 4 = \boxed{5}$

$12 - 8 = \boxed{4}$

$7 - 2 = \boxed{5}$

$13 - 12 = \boxed{1}$

$20 - 10 = \boxed{10}$

$18 - 9 = \boxed{9}$

$16 - 4 = \boxed{12}$

$4 - 2 = \boxed{2}$

$7 - 1 = \boxed{6}$

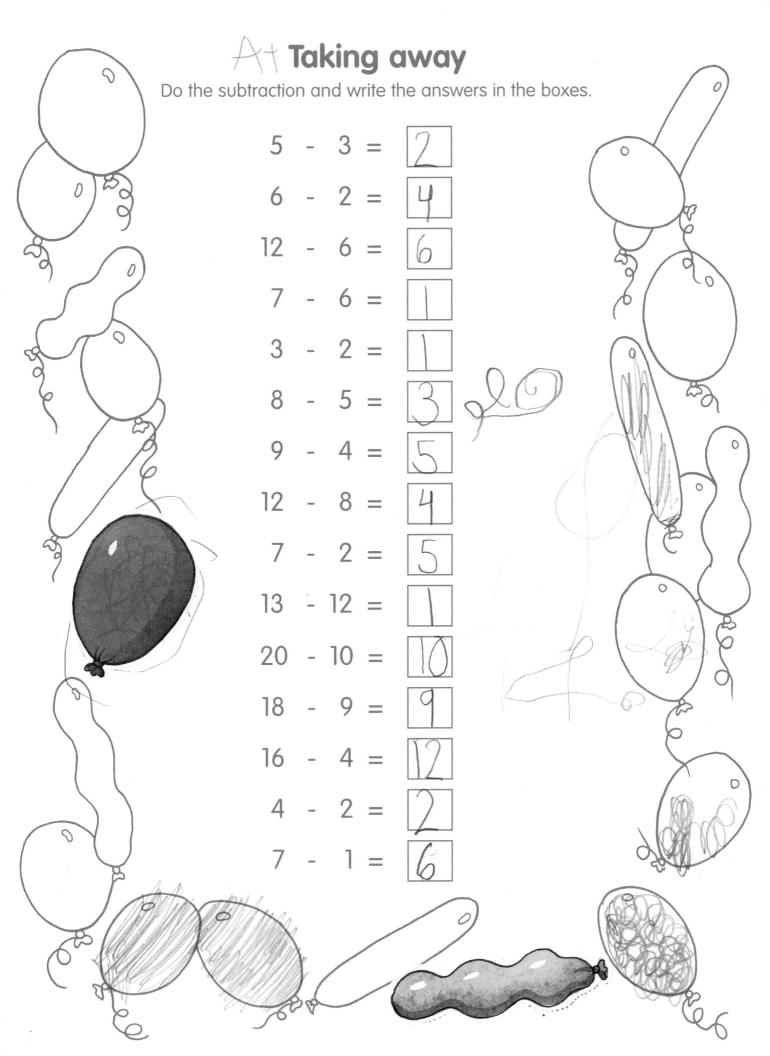

Missing numbers

Look at the problems on the buckets—the answers are missing.
Each elephant is holding a bun with his trunk. Write the answers on the buns.

4 + 2 =

4 + 6 =

10 − 3 =

8 − 6 =

Flower addition

Find the stickers and put them in place. Count the flowers and write the number on the vase. Do the addition and write the final answers in the boxes.

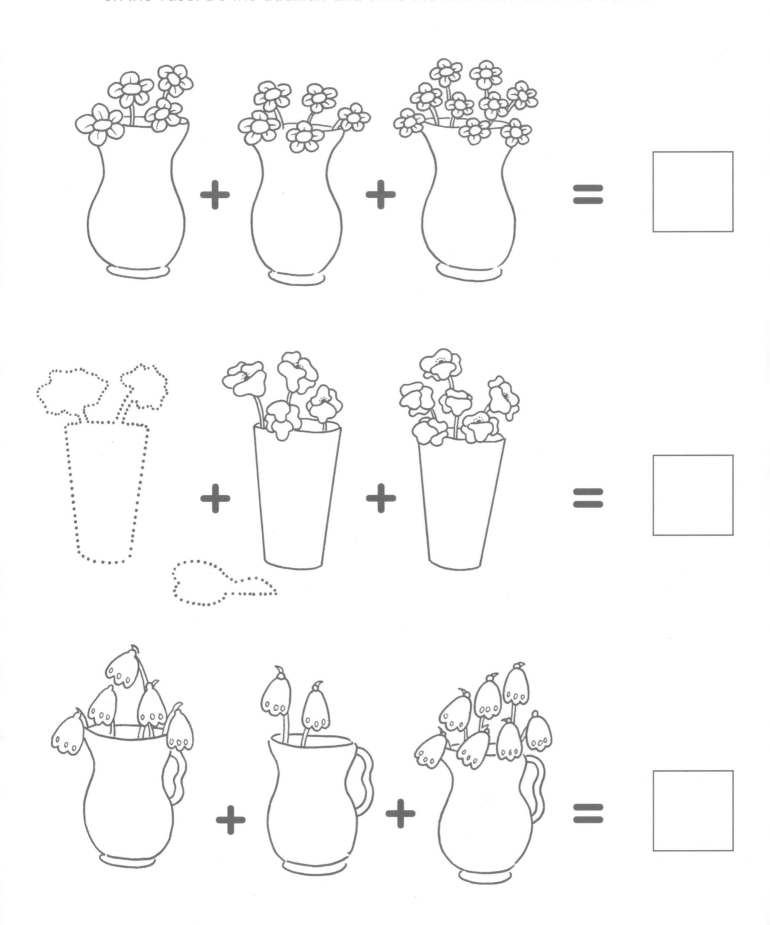

Number puzzles

Complete the problems in the grids by filling in
the missing numbers.

6	−		=	4
+		−		+
	+	1	=	5
=		=		=
10	−	1	=	

	+	7	=	10
−		−		−
2	+		=	5
=		=		=
1	+	4	=	

Math wordsearch

Do the math.
The answers are written as words in the
wordsearch grid. Circle the words as you find them.
Use the words in the word bank to help you.

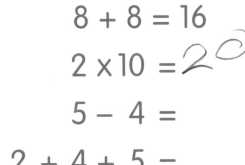

$8 + 8 = 16$

$2 \times 10 = 20$

$5 - 4 =$

$2 + 4 + 5 =$

$10 - 6 - 2 =$

$15 - 12 =$

| TWENTY | ONE | SIXTEEN |
| THREE | ELEVEN | TWO |

F S I O A W E E O
I I H T I O J L M
N X V C X Z A E D
F T W E N T Y V I
U E T R I W Q E S
Z E C D P O F N B
O N E H E M J U I
O K L I O I J H B
V D F R T G H Y U
I J K M T H R E E

Count and copy

Look at the example. Find the stickers and put them in place.
Copy and draw the right number of things to finish the problems.

Example:

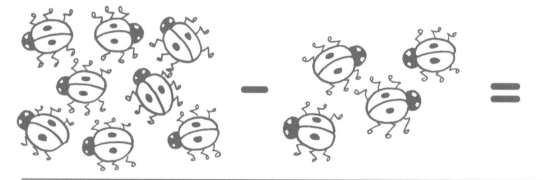

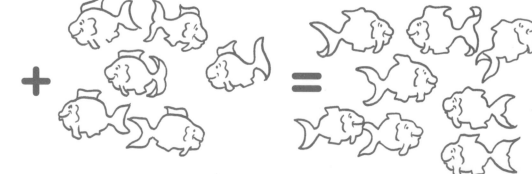

Groups

Find the stickers and put them in place. There are 20 pieces of candy on this page. Separate the candy into groups of four pieces. Draw a circle around each group. Write the answer on the jar.

Number lines

Look at the example and draw lines to connect each balloon to the right place on the line.

Example:

| 0 | 5 | 10 | 15 | 20 | 25 | 30 | 35 |

Math wordsearch

Do the math. The answers are written as words in the
wordsearch grid. Circle the words as you find them.
Use the words in the word bank to help you.

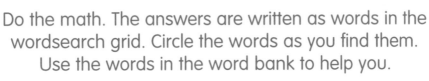

$$5 + 4 = 9$$

$$15 + 3 =$$

$$12 - 4 =$$

$$3 + 5 + 2 =$$

$$20 - 6 - 7 =$$

$$20 - 12 - 2 =$$

TEN	EIGHT	EIGHTEEN
SEVEN	NINE	SIX

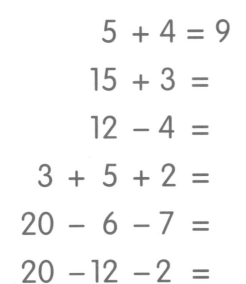

T	T	E	N	H	Y	T	P	D
N	M	I	P	S	K	O	S	H
G	F	G	E	E	Y	U	I	U
H	N	H	V	V	F	R	X	W
Q	A	T	X	E	V	B	N	M
K	L	E	O	N	U	J	H	Y
T	R	E	D	E	W	E	R	F
B	N	N	I	N	E	U	T	F
C	Z	X	Z	A	W	F	O	I
A	W	E	R	E	I	G	H	T

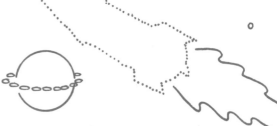

Number snakes

The numbers in each snake form a sequence.
Fill in the missing numbers.

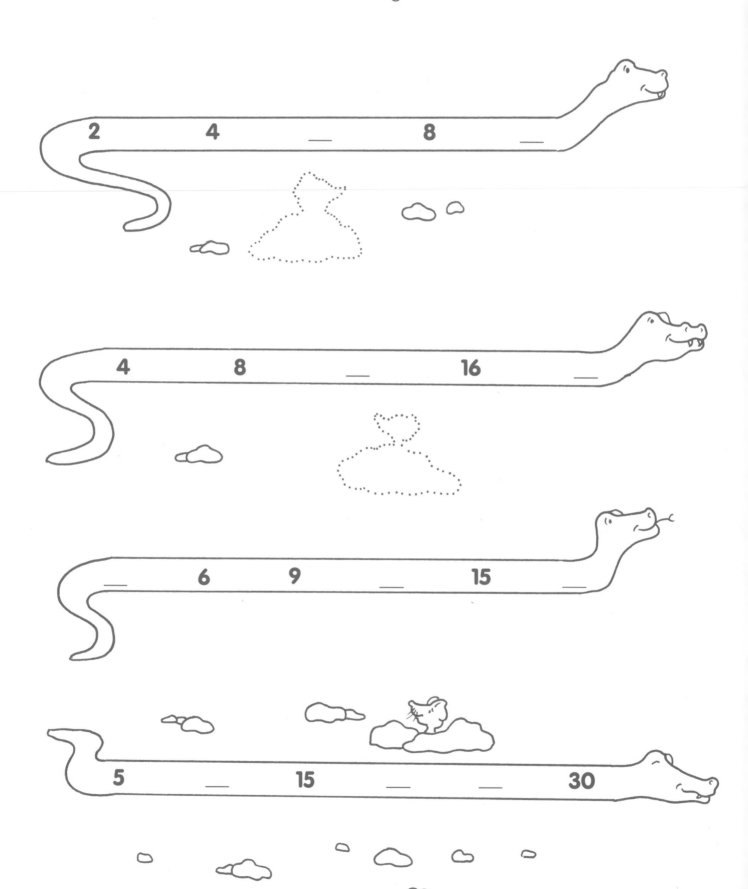

2   4   __   8   __

4   8   __   16   __

__   6   9   __   15   __

5   __   15   __   __   30

Number puzzles

Do the problems in the grids by filling in the missing numbers.

	−	3	=	5
+	■	+	■	+
2	−		=	1
=	■	=	■	=
10	−	4	=	

7	−	3	=	
+	■	−	■	+
	+	2	=	5
=	■	=	■	=
10	−		=	9

Odds and evens

Find the stickers and put them in place. Count the chicks in each group.
Check the box if you think there is an odd number. Put a cross in the box if you
think there is an even number.

Number patterns

Find the stickers and put them in place.
Look carefully at the patterns and fill in the missing numbers.

1	2	3	4	5	6	7	8	9	10

1   4   2

          7   9

                    2   1

               6   10

Answers

Shortest and tallest
The girl is the shortest.
The tree is the tallest.

Groups
There are 4 groups.

Count and add
There are 9 spots on the butterflies' wings.

Shapes
There are 2 long balloons.
There are 2 round balloons.
There are 3 oval balloons.
There are 3 wavy balloons.

Most and fewest
e has the most   b has the fewest

Adding
$3 + 1 = 4$ $3 + 2 = 5$
$3 + 3 = 6$ $3 + 4 = 7$

Squirrel subtraction
$20 - 16 = 4$ $30 - 22 = 8$
$15 - 13 = 2$ $12 - 7 = 5$

Shapes
There are 10 triangles. There are 9 squares.
There are 8 ovals. There are 6 rectangles.

Adding
$1 + 2 = 3$ $6 + 5 = 11$ $8 + 1 = 9$
$3 + 3 = 6$ $4 + 8 = 12$ $2 + 10 = 12$
$3 + 5 = 8$ $9 + 3 = 12$ $6 + 8 = 14$
$10 + 10 = 20$ $4 + 4 = 8$ $2 + 12 = 14$
$8 + 8 = 16$ $9 + 9 = 18$ $10 + 11 = 21$

Count and add
There are 28 markings on the cows.

Matching answers
$5 + 5 = 10$ $15 - 6 = 9$ $14 + 2 = 16$

Taking away
$5 - 3 = 2$ $6 - 2 = 4$ $12 - 6 = 6$
$7 - 6 = 1$ $3 - 2 = 1$ $8 - 5 = 3$
$9 - 4 = 5$ $12 - 8 = 4$ $7 - 2 = 5$
$13 - 12 = 1$ $20 - 10 = 10$ $18 - 9 = 9$
$16 - 4 = 12$ $4 - 2 = 2$ $7 - 1 = 6$

Missing numbers
$4 + 2 = 6$ $4 + 6 = 10$ $10 - 3 = 7$ $8 - 6 = 2$

Flower addition
$4 + 5 + 9 = 18$ $2 + 4 + 6 = 12$ $5 + 2 + 7 = 14$

Number puzzles

6	−	2	=	4
+		−		+
4	+	1	=	5
=		=		=
10	−	1	=	9

3	+	7	=	10
−		−		−
2	+	3	=	5
=		=		=
1	+	4	=	5

Math wordsearch

F	S	I	O	A	W	E	E	O
I	I	H	T	I	O	J	L	M
N	X	V	C	X	Z	A	E	D
F	T	W	E	N	T	Y	V	I
U	E	T	R	I	W	Q	E	S
Z	E	C	D	P	O	F	N	B
O	N	E	H	E	M	J	U	I
O	K	L	I	O	I	J	H	B
V	D	F	R	T	G	H	Y	U
I	J	K	M	T	H	R	E	E

Count and copy
6 snails - 3 snails = 3 snails
8 ladybugs - 4 ladybugs = 4 ladybugs
14 apples - 5 apples = 9 apples
2 fish + 6 fish = 8 fish

Groups
There are 5 groups.

Math wordsearch

T	T	E	N	H	Y	T	P	D
N	M	I	P	S	K	O	S	H
G	F	G	E	E	Y	U	I	U
H	N	H	V	V	F	R	X	W
Q	A	T	X	E	V	B	N	M
K	L	E	O	N	U	J	H	Y
T	R	E	D	E	W	E	R	F
B	N	N	I	N	E	U	T	F
C	Z	X	Z	A	W	F	O	I
A	W	E	R	E	I	G	H	T

Number snakes
2 4 6 8 10   4 8 12 16 20
3 6 9 12 15 18   5 10 15 20 25 30

Number puzzles

8	−	3	=	5
+		+		+
2	−	1	=	1
=		=		=
10	−	4	=	6

7	−	3	=	4
+		−		+
3	+	2	=	5
=		=		=
10	−	1	=	9

Number patterns
1 4 3 5 2   8 7 10 9 6
7 4 2 10 1   2 4 6 8 10

Phonics

Especially suitable for grades K-2

First letter sounds

Find the stickers and put them in place.
Write the first letter to complete each word.

_all

_nchor

_ar

_lephant

_uck

_ish

_at

_ate

_gloo

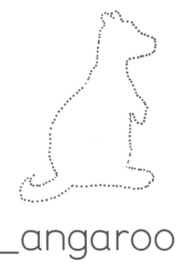

_angaroo

_eep

_ion

More first letter sounds

Find the stickers and put them in place.
Write the first letter to complete each word.

_urse

_oon

_range

_uilt

_anda

_abbit

_able

_mbrella

_ock

_ase

_atch

_-ray

_o-yo

_ebra

First letter exercises

Find the stickers and put them in place. Draw a line under each picture that has the same first sound as the letter at the beginning of the line.
Look carefully—sometimes there's more than one.

Last letter sounds

Find the stickers and put them in place.
Write the last letter to complete each word. Use the pictures to help you.

we_b

bir_d

fro_g

bal_

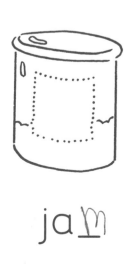

ja_m

hen

mop

star

cat

fox

Last sounds exercises

Find the stickers and put them in place.
Write the last letter to complete each word.

te_   pe_   su_

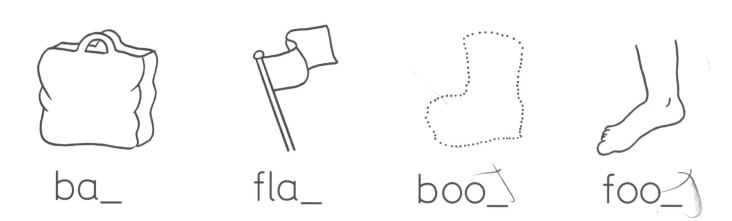

ba_   fla_   boo_   foo_

goa_   bir_   han_

More last sounds exercises

Find the stickers and put them in place.
Find the pictures that end with the letter in each box.
Color them red.

First and last letter sounds

Find the stickers and put them in place. The first and last letters are missing.
Write the letters to complete the words. Use the pictures to help you.

_oo_

_ir_

low

_oa_

_o_

_u_

_oo_

_uc_

emo

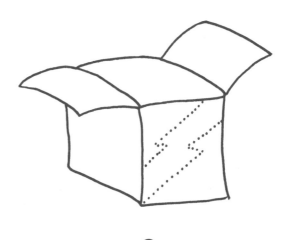

_o_

Middle letter sounds

Find the stickers and put them in place. The middle letters are missing from these words.
Write the missing letters to complete the words.
The missing letters are all vowels—a, e, i, o, and u. Use the pictures to help you.

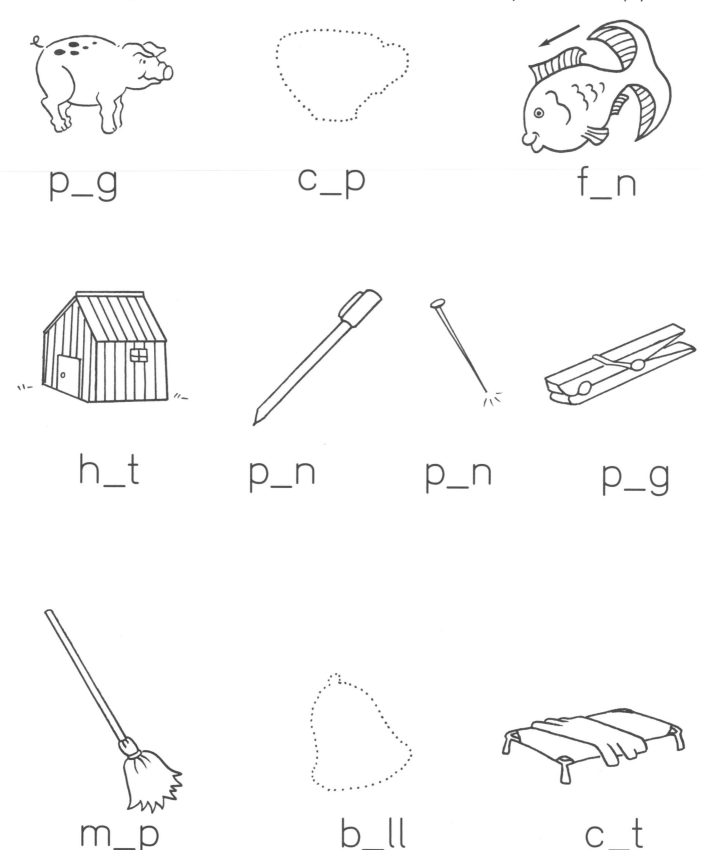

p_g

c_p

f_n

h_t

p_n

p_n

p_g

m_p

b_ll

c_t

Middle letter sounds exercises

Find the stickers and put them in place. Write the missing letters.
Draw a line to match the words that rhyme.

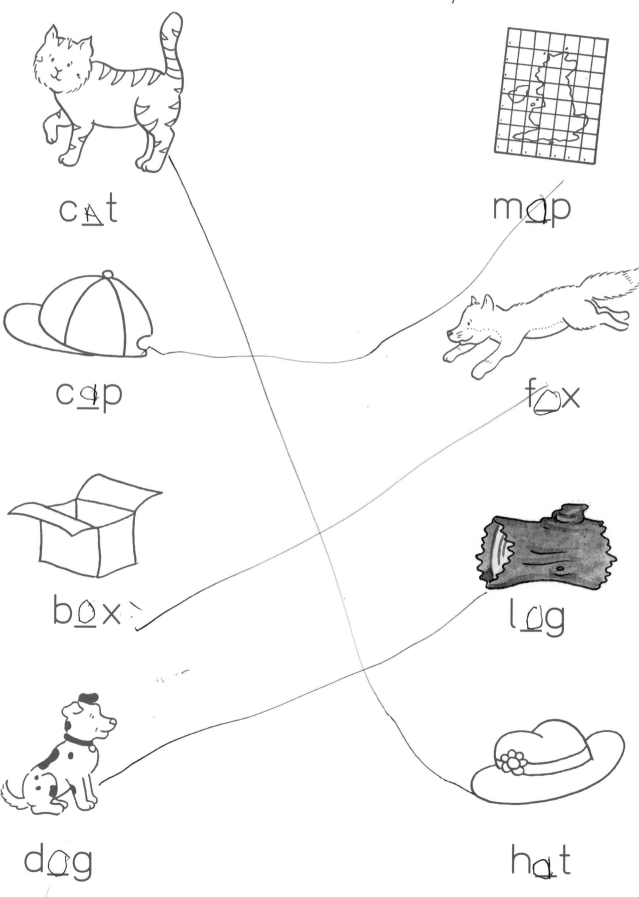

c_a_t

m_a_p

c_a_p

f_o_x

b_o_x

l_o_g

d_o_g

h_a_t

Rhyming words

Find the stickers and put them in place. Look at the pictures in each group
of rhyming words and write the first letter to complete the words.
The letters you will write are called consonants.

_at   _at   _at

_en   _en   _en

_ing   _ing   _ing

_ock

_lock

_ock

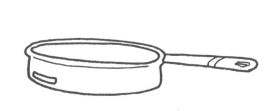

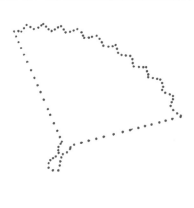

_an

_an

_an

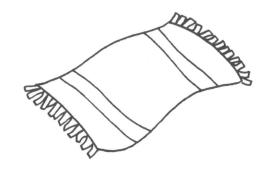

_ug

_ug

_ug

Rhyming words exercises

Find the stickers and put them in place. Look at the pictures in each set.
The words for two pictures rhyme. Draw a line to connect them,
and circle the rhyming words in the boxes.

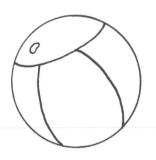

ball

butterfly

wall

flower

chair

mat

book

vase

cat

apple

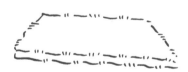

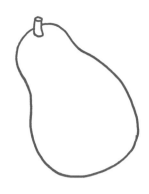

pear
hat
fish
dish
yarn

---

mitten
ladder
scissors
kitten
clock

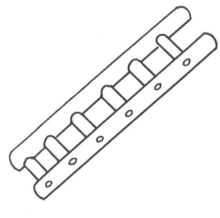

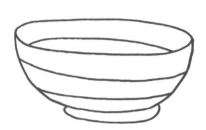

Sound patterns

Find the stickers and put them in place. Sometimes double letters are used to make a longer sound. These can be vowels or consonants. Write the missing letters to complete the words.

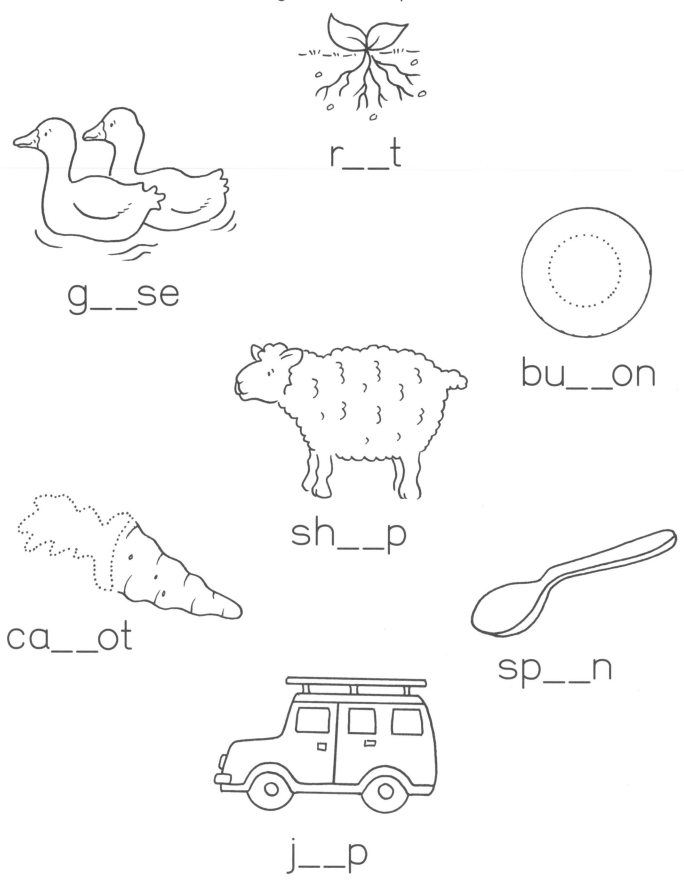

r__t

g__se

bu__on

sh__p

ca__ot

sp__n

j__p

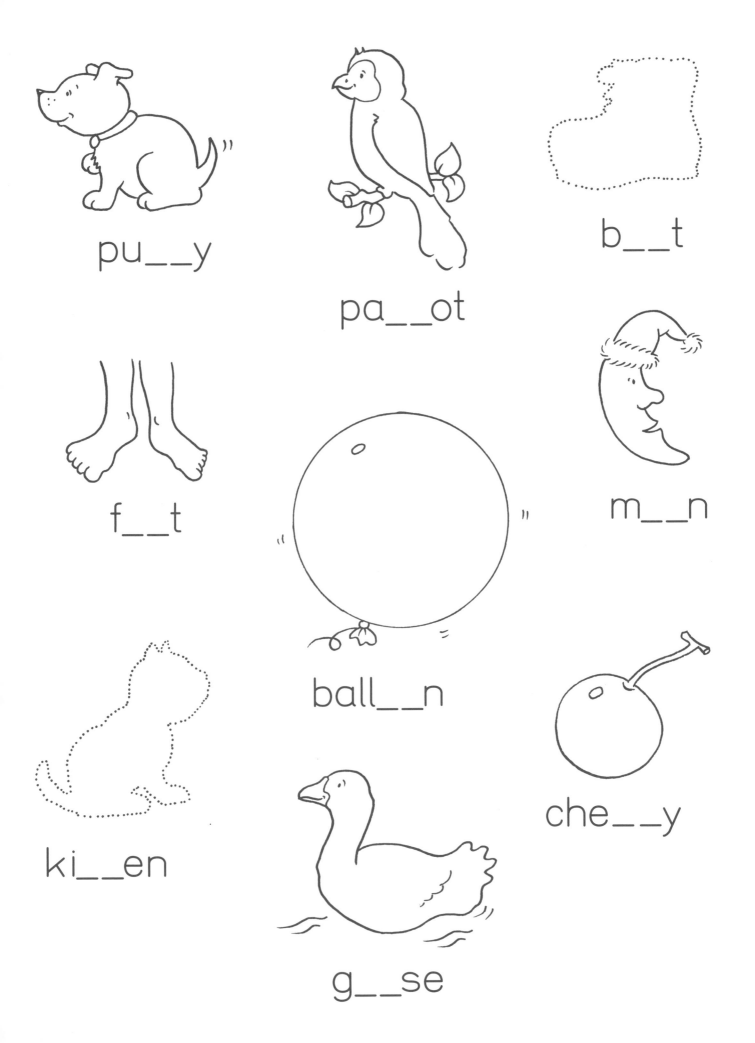

pu__y

pa__ot

b__t

f__t

ball__n

m__n

ki__en

g__se

che__y

More sound patterns

Find the stickers and put them in place. Two different vowels can be used together to make a sound. Sometimes this makes a longer sound, but not always. Write the missing letters to complete the words.

ea

l__f   p__ch   __gle

ou

h__se   cl__d   f__ntain

ow

cl__n   t__el   sh__er

ai

tr__n   p__nt   sn__l

oa

b__t   g__t   s__p

Double last letters

Find the stickers and put them in place.
Some words have double letters at the end to make a longer sound.
Write the missing letters to complete the words.

ba＿＿   e＿＿   we＿＿

gla＿＿   b＿＿   z＿＿

Double last letters exercises

Find the stickers and put them in place. Complete the words in the box.
Write each word on the line under the correct picture.

_____

_____

_____

_____

_____

_____

she _____

tr _____

dre _____

hi _____

be _____

kangar _____

Silent e

Find the stickers and put them in place. The letter **e** at the end of a word changes the sound of the vowels. Look at the example, then add an **e** to each word.

Example:

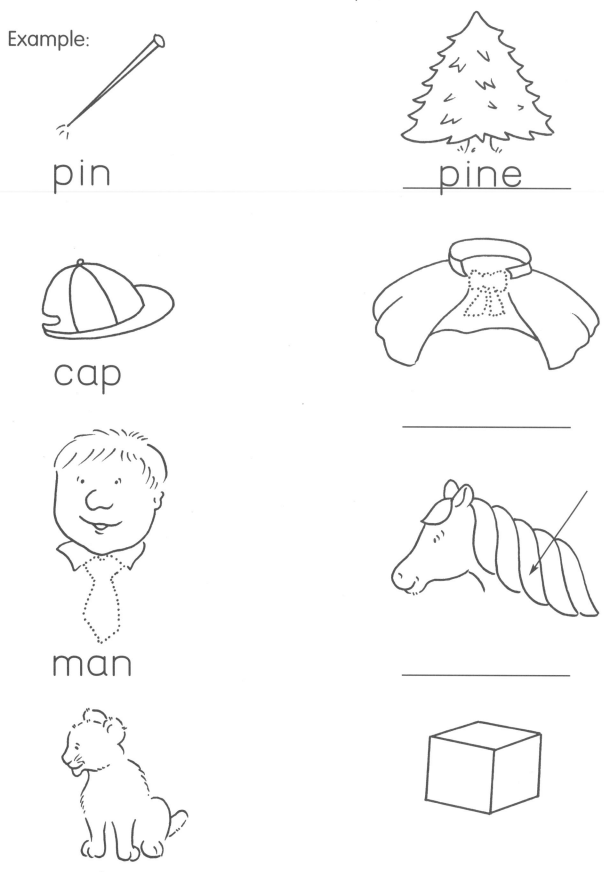

pin

pine

cap

_____

man

_____

cub

_____

Silent e or not?

Find the stickers and put them in place. Add an **e** where you can.
Put an **x** through the words where an **e** cannot be added to make a word.

fish

pip

hen

pig

tub

map

tap

Words that sound the same

Find the stickers and put them in place. Look at the example.
Some words sound the same but have different spellings.
Look at the words in the boxes and write words that sound the same.
Use the pictures to help you.

Example:

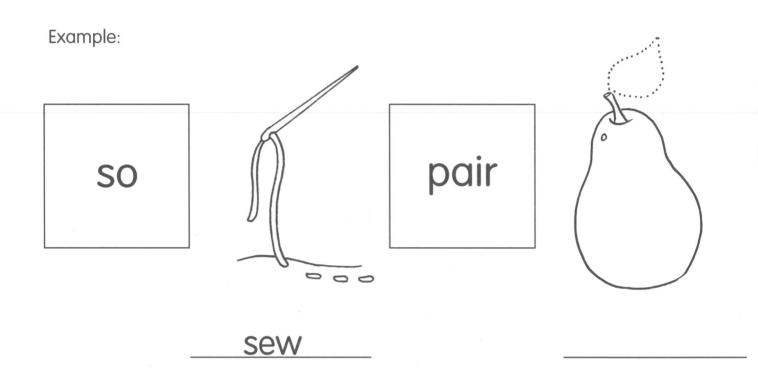

so		pair	

___sew___

_____

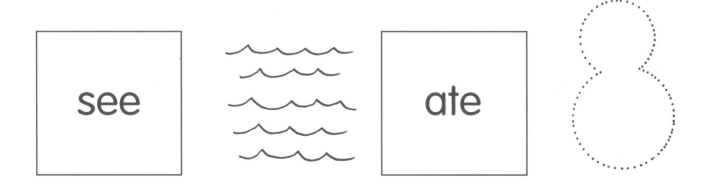

see		ate	

_____   _____

Wordsearch

Find the stickers and put them in place. The words under the pictures are hidden in the grid. You will find them by reading across or down. Circle the words as you find them.

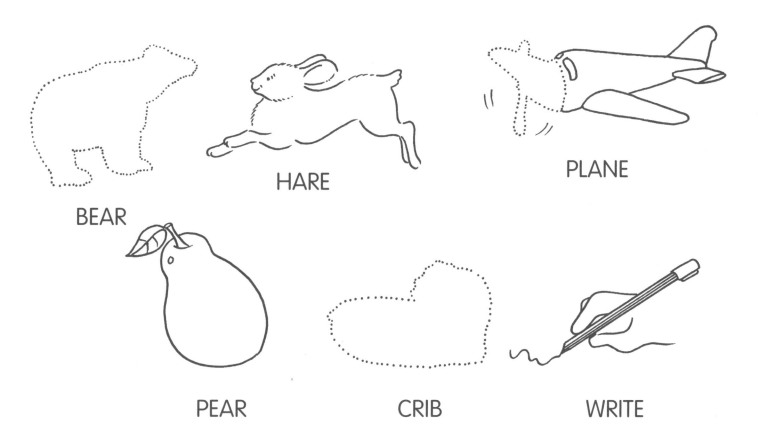

BEAR

HARE

PLANE

PEAR

CRIB

WRITE

B	X	S	U	A	X	C	I	Q
E	Z	G	N	P	F	K	F	M
A	T	K	B	L	U	A	X	S
R	R	S	H	A	R	E	W	K
U	Q	C	A	D	R	G	R	U
P	E	A	R	I	I	O	I	P
L	K	P	T	L	Z	L	T	K
A	F	A	B	U	P	U	E	P
N	J	S	C	R	I	B	Q	A
E	I	C	X	T	D	R	I	B

Answers

First letter sounds
anchor   ball   car
duck   elephant   fish
gate   hat   igloo
jeep   kangaroo   lion

More first letter sounds
moon   nurse   orange
panda   quilt   rabbit
sock   table   umbrella
vase   watch   x-ray   yo-yo   zebra

First letter exercises

a = ant	n = nose
b = baby	o = octopus
c = cat	p = pan
d = dolphin	q = queen
and dog	r = rake
e = egg	s = snail and sun
f = fork	t = turtle
g = goat	u = umbrella
h = hat	v = violin
i = ink	w = watch
j = jar	x = xylophone
k = kite	y = yo-yo
l = lamb	z = zebra
m = moon	

Last letter sounds
web   bird   frog   ball   jar
hen   mop   star   cat   fox

Last sounds exercises
ten   pen   sun   bag   flag
boot   foot   goat   bird   hand

More last sounds excercise
t = boat and hat   m = arm
p = cup   x = box and six

First and last letter sounds
moon   bird   clown   boat   fox
cup   book   duck   lemon   box

Middle letter sounds
pig   cup   fin   hut   pen
pin   peg   mop   bell   cot

Middle letter sounds exercises
cat - hat   cap - map

box - fox   dog - log

Rhyming words
bat   hat   rat
hen   pen   ten
ring   king   wing
rock   clock   sock
pan   man   fan
rug   bug   mug

Rhyming words exercises
ball - wall   mat - cat
fish - dish   mitten - kitten

Sound patterns
geese   root   button   carrot
sheep   spoon   jeep
puppy   parrot   boot
feet   balloon   moon
kitten   goose   cherry

More sound patterns
leaf   peach   eagle
house   cloud   fountain
clown   towel   shower
train   paint   snail
boat   goat   soap

Double last letters
ball   egg   well
glass   bee   zoo

Double last letters exercises
shell   tree   dress   hill   bell   kangaroo

Silent e
cap - cape   man - mane   cub - cube

Silent e or not?
pipe   tube   tape

Words that sound the same
sew - so   pear - pair
sea - see   eight - ate

Wordsearch

Tell the Time

Especially suitable for grades K-2

Before or after?

Find the stickers and put them in place. Write the answer in the box.

A

before

Do you turn on the water **before** or **after** you wash your hands?

B

after

Do you wash the dishes **before** or **after** a meal?

C

after

Do you cheer **before** or **after** someone scores a goal?

D

before

Do you put a leash on a dog **before** or **after** you take it for a walk?

Less time

Find the stickers and put them in place. Look at these pictures carefully.
Which do you think takes **less** time? Check the box.

Which do you think takes **less** time? Check the box.

brushing your
teeth

painting a
house

More time

Find the stickers and put them in place. Look at these pictures carefully.
Which do you think takes **more** time? Check the box.

doing a somersault ☐

climbing a mountain ☒

Which do you think takes **more** time? Check the box.

feeding the cat ☐

tidying up your room

Ship ahoy!

Compare the pictures and look for the differences between day and night.
Find the sun and moon stickers and write "day" or "night" under each picture.

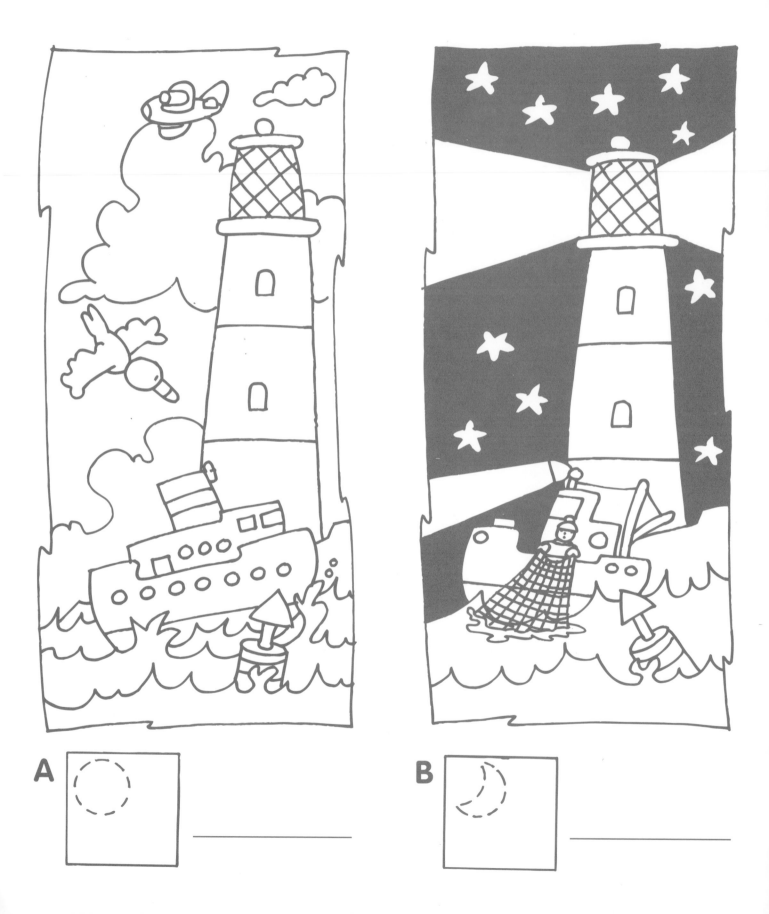

A

B

Puppy playmates

Compare the pictures and look for the differences between day and night.
Find the sun and moon stickers and write "day" or "night" under each picture.

A _____

B _____

Clock face

There are 12 numbers on a clock face. Find the number stickers and put them in their places around the clock face.

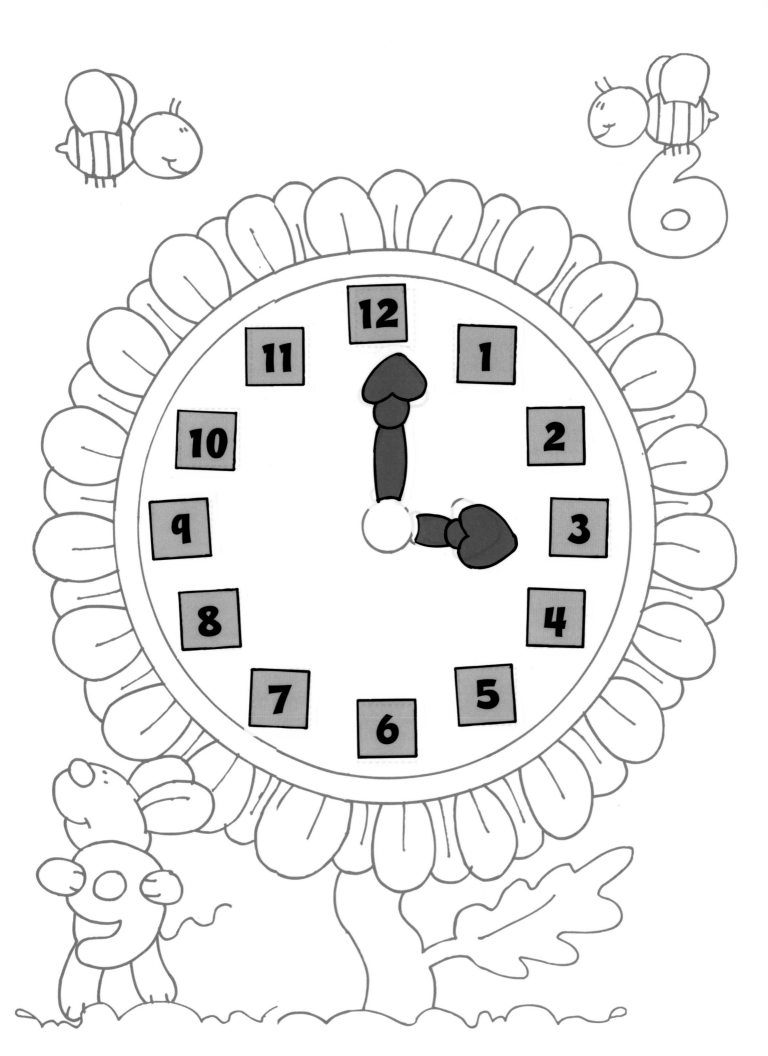

Clock hands

The hands on a clock face show you the time by pointing to numbers.
The number the **short hand** points to shows the **hour**.
The number the **long hand** points to shows the **minutes**.

Find the blue short-hand sticker and point it to the number 9.
Then find the blue long-hand sticker and point it to the number 12.
This shows you that it is 9 o'clock.

Practice 1

Look at the times in the boxes under each clock.
Draw hands on the clock faces so that they tell the times in the boxes.
Use the example to help you.

Example:

1 o'clock

3 o'clock

5 o'clock

8 o'clock

11 o'clock

12 o'clock

Time wordsearch

Find the time words in the wordsearch grid. You will find them by reading across or down.
Circle the words as you find them.

| TIME | FACE | HOURS | NUMBERS |
| CLOCK | HANDS | MINUTES | |

```
A  K  F  L  O  I  N  J  K
J  H  A  N  D  S  K  B  P
L  M  C  H  Y  I  P  H  M
M  L  E  A  T  R  S  O  Y
I  I  Y  U  I  T  E  U  M
N  R  N  U  M  B  E  R  S
U  L  O  P  E  I  T  S  Y
T  L  M  I  U  T  Y  R  F
E  P  B  I  U  M  D  R  E
S  T  E  C  L  O  C  K  L
```

Morning, afternoon, evening, or night

Do these pictures show morning, afternoon, evening, or night time?
Find the stickers and put them in place.

A

B

morning

5 2 6

afternoon evening night

What time is it?

Find the stickers that tell the times shown on each of these clocks.

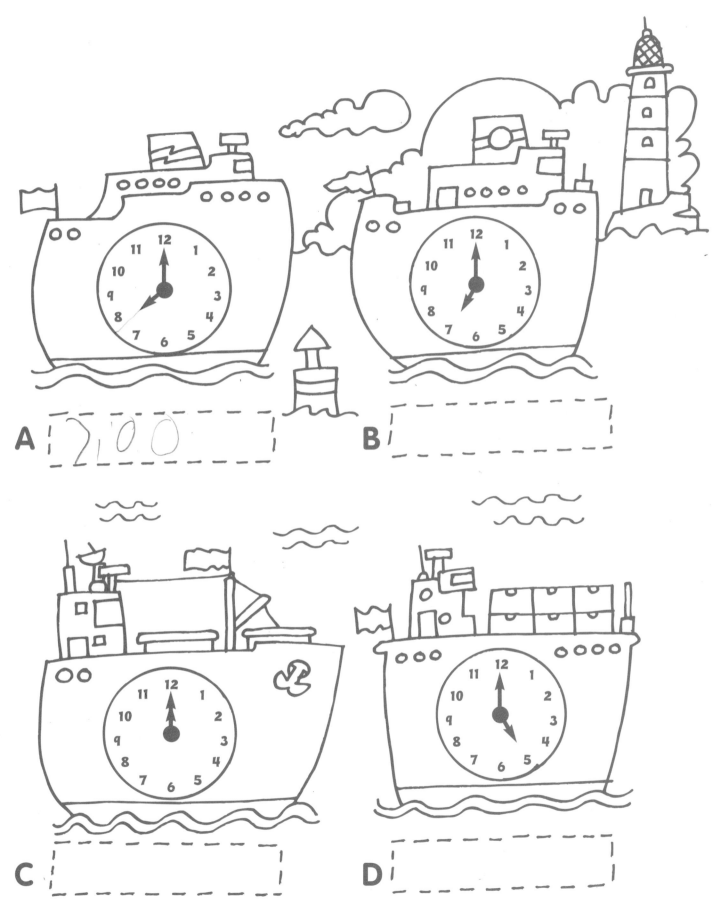

A 2:00

B

C

D

Half an hour

Like a pizza, a clock face can be cut into two halves or four quarters.
There are 30 minutes in half an hour.

halves

half an hour
(30 minutes)

Quarter of an hour

There are 15 minutes in a quarter of an hour.

quarters

quarter of an hour
(15 minutes)

Half past

When the long hand points to the number 6, it is half past an hour.
Find the yellow long-hand sticker and point it to 6. Then find the yellow short-hand sticker
and point it halfway between 2 and 3. This shows it is half past two.

half past two

Quarter after

When the long hand points to the number 3, it is a quarter after an hour.
Find the red long-hand sticker and point it to 3.
Then find the red short-hand sticker and point it to just past 10.
This shows it is a quarter after ten.

a quarter after ten

Quarter to

When the long hand points to the number 9, it is a quarter to an hour.
Find the green long-hand sticker and point it to 9. Then find the green short-hand
sticker and point it almost to 5. This shows it is a quarter to five.

a quarter to five

Practice 2

Look at the times on these clocks. Find the stickers that match the times.

Look at the times in the boxes. Draw the missing hands on these clock faces.

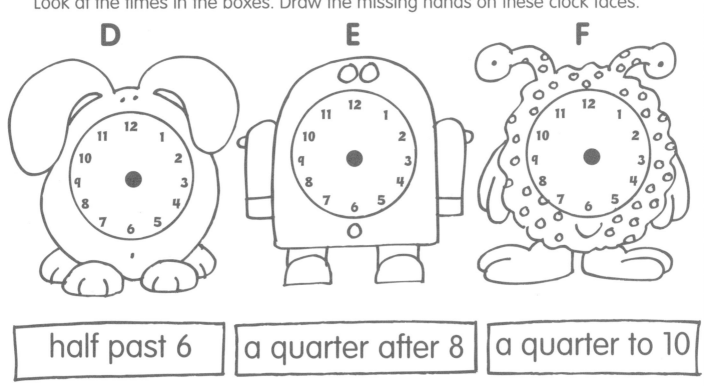

half past 6

a quarter after 8

a quarter to 10

Snail's pace

Find the stickers and put them in place. Which snail gets to the top of the flower first?
Find out which snail wins the race by adding the number 5s together.
The snail with the lowest number wins!

A

B

Face to face

Draw lines to match the clocks to their missing clock faces.

A

B

C

D

1   2   3   4

What time?

Find the stickers and put them in place.
Look at each picture and draw the missing hands on each clock
to show what time you might do these things.

Numbers wordsearch

Look in the wordsearch grid for the number words between 1 and 12.
You will find them by reading across or down.
Circle the words as you find them.

R	T	W	O	A	I	S	I	X
W	H	P	K	I	E	T	R	E
N	R	H	T	T	S	E	D	R
L	E	L	E	V	E	N	T	F
N	E	R	N	T	V	K	Y	I
F	O	U	R	T	E	E	R	V
M	I	O	U	T	N	I	N	E
N	U	N	Y	E	R	G	W	E
T	W	E	L	V	E	H	T	E
H	T	G	R	E	M	T	P	V

Tell me the time

Look at the clocks below. One clock shows the time using hands.
The other clock shows the time using only numbers.
What is the time on each clock?

At one o' clock

Practice 3

Look at the times on the round clock faces and find the number clock stickers that tell the same time. A+

Look at the times on the number clocks and draw the missing hands on the round clock faces to show the same time. finish

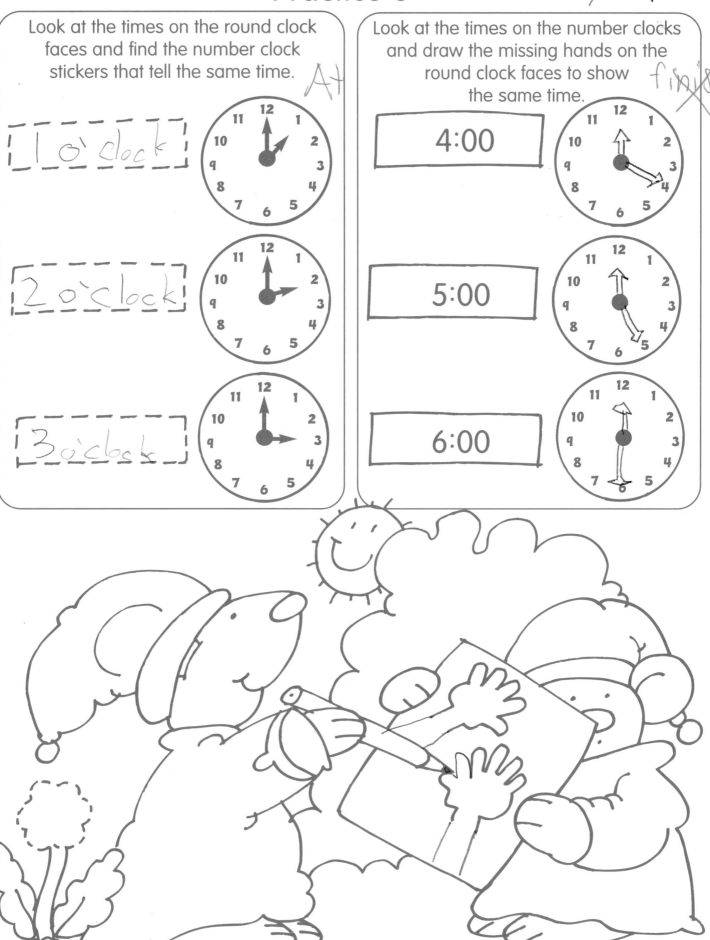

1 o'clock

2 o'clock

3 o'clock

4:00

5:00

6:00

Answers

Before or after?
A before   B after
C after   D before

Less time
A falling acorn takes less time.
Brushing your teeth takes less time.

More time
Climbing a mountain takes more time.
Tidying up your room takes more time.

Ship ahoy!
A day   B night

Puppy playmates
A day   B night

Clock hands

Practice 1
3 o'clock   5 o'clock   8 o'clock   11 o'clock   12 o'clock

Time wordsearch

Morning, afternoon, evening, or night
A morning   B afternoon
C evening   D night

Adding fives
15, 20, 25, 30, 35, 40, 45, 50, 55, 60

What time is it?
A 8 o'clock   B 7 o'clock
C 12 o'clock   D 5 o'clock

Half past

Quarter after

Quarter to

Practice 2
A half past 3   B a quarter after 2
C a quarter to 4

    D   E   F

Snail's pace
A - 25, B - 35 snail A wins

Face to face
A - 4 B - 1 C - 3 D - 2

Numbers wordsearch

Tell me the time
1 o'clock

Practice 3
A 1:00   B 2:00   C 3:00

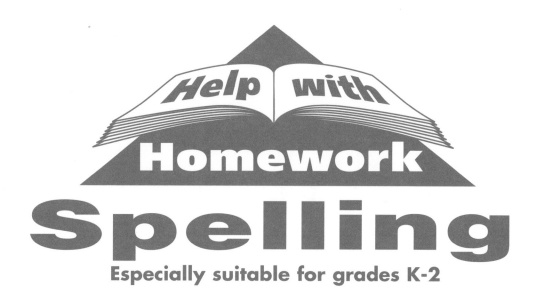

Spelling

Especially suitable for grades K-2

Which pet?

Find the stickers and put them in place.
Follow the leashes to find out which pet belongs to which child.

First letter

Find the stickers and put them in place. Starting with **a**, work through the alphabet and write the first letters to spell the words.

__nt   __us   __at

__uck   __gg   __ish

__oat   __at   __nk

__ar   __ite   __amb

__oon

__est

__ctopus

__enguin

__ueen

__ose

__un

__iger

__mbrella

__ase

__eb

__-ray

__o-yo

__ebra

Last letter

Find the stickers and put them in place.
Look at the picture with each word and write the last letter.

cra__

be__

lea__

ba__

ca__

snai__

ja__

he__

cherr__

to__

ca__

bo__

Last letter sounds

Look at the pictures and the words under them.

ink

boat

train

sheep

clown

bell

How many words end with **n**? Write them on the line.

_____

How many words end with **p**? Write them on the line.

_____

How many words end with **k**? Write them on the line.

_____

What's wrong here?

Find the stickers and put them in place. Look carefully at this picture.
There are 10 things wrong—can you find them?

Words with a

Find the stickers and put them in place. Look at the pictures and the words under them.
Add the letter **a** to complete the words in the box.

man   cap   baby   jam   lamp

apple   hat   cat   fan   pan

_pple   c_p   c__t

h__t   b_by   l__mp

Words with e

Find the stickers and put them in place. Look at the pictures and the words under them.
Add the letter **e** to complete the words in the box.

tent   hen   bell   teddy

well   bed   vest   pen

t_nt   h_n   t_ddy

p_n   b_d

Words with i

Find the stickers and put them in place.
Look at the pictures, then add the letter **i** to complete these words.

pin   king   hill   pig   kitten

p_g   k_ng   k_tten

Words with o

Find the stickers and put them in place.
Look at the pictures, then add the letter **o** to complete these words.

fox   doll   dog   pot   top

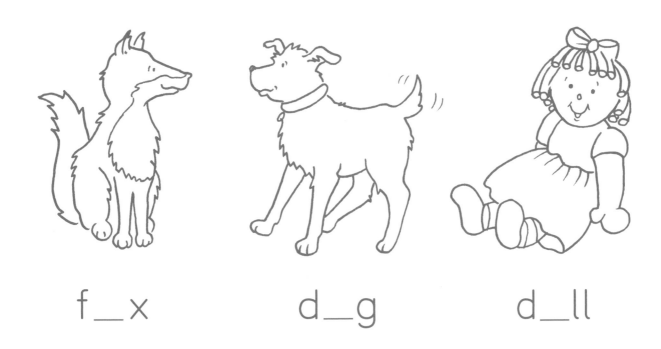

f__x   d__g   d__ll

Words with u

Find the stickers and put them in place.
Look at the pictures, then add the letter **u** to complete these words.

cup   umbrella   sun   puppy

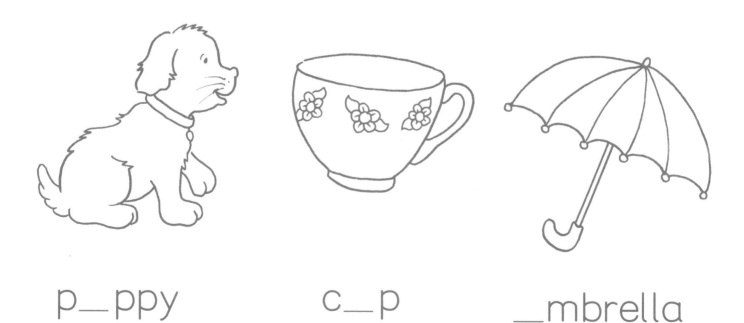

p_ppy   c_p   _mbrella

Words with a e i o u

Find the stickers and put them in place. The letters **a e i o** and **u** are called vowels. All the other letters in the alphabet are called consonants. Look at the pictures, then add the letters **a e i o** or **u** to complete the words. Write the words on the lines.

b_by

_gg

k_tten

d_ll

p_ppy

Something beginning with s

Find the stickers and put them in place.
How many things can you find in the picture that begin with the letter **s**?

Match the words

Some words in the balloons are the same, and some look similar.
Draw lines to match the words that are the same. Then, color the balloons.

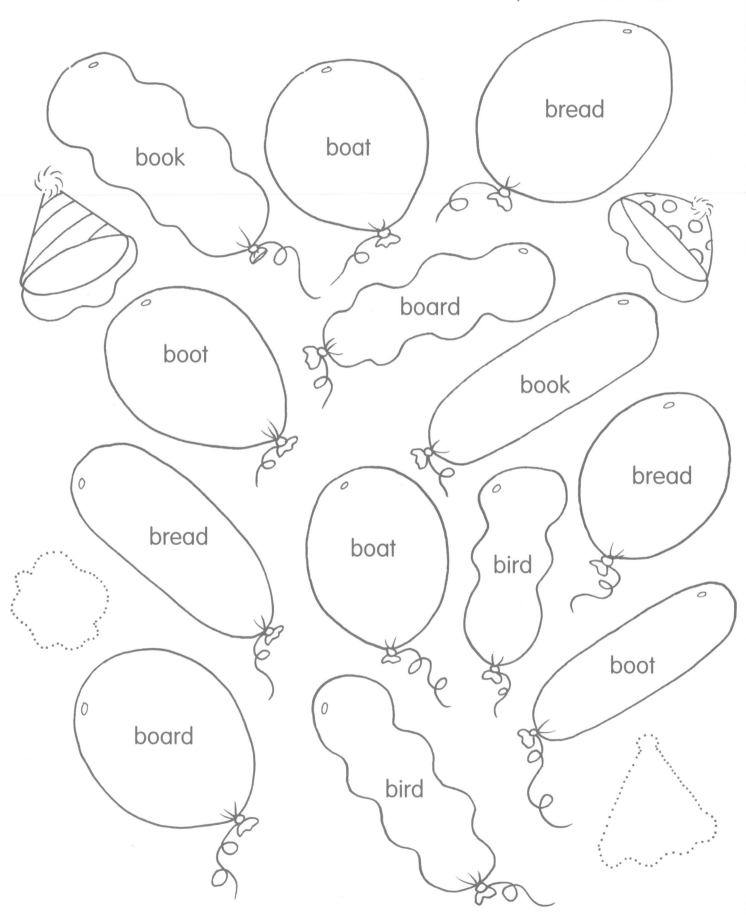

The sound ou and ow

Ou and **ow** can make the same sound even though they use different letters. Match the words that have the same sound and color them the same color.

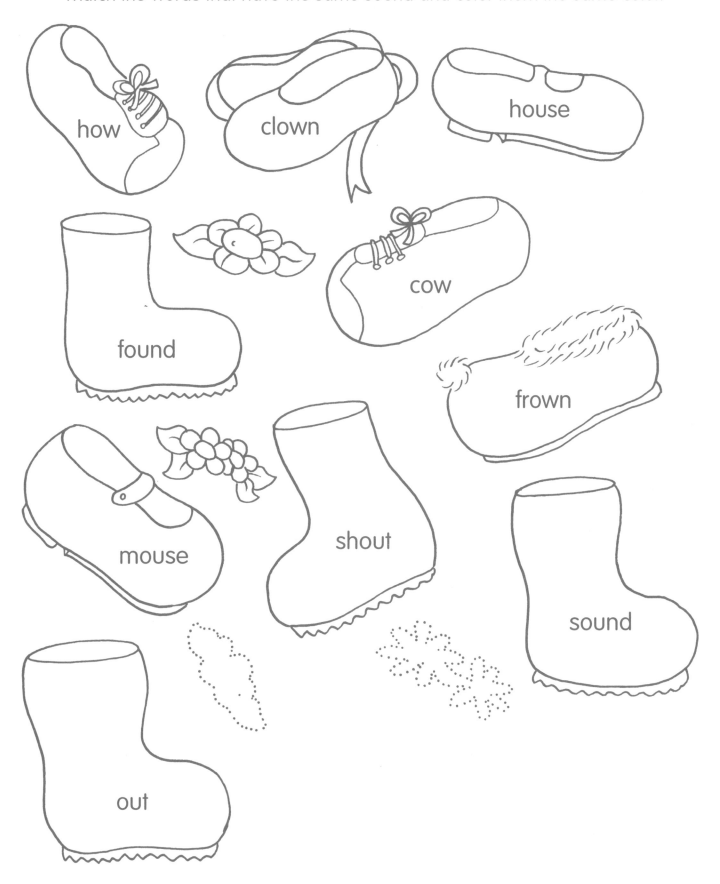

Adding e

The letter **e** at the end of a word changes the sound of the vowel.
Look at the example, then add an **e** to the words.

Example:

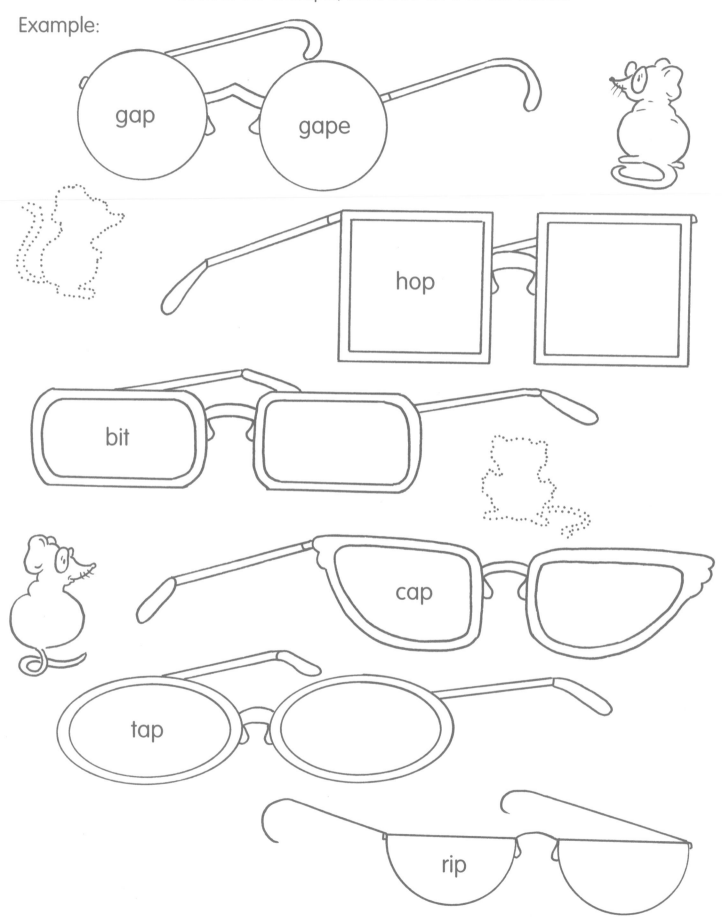

gap

gape

hop

bit

cap

tap

rip

Double letters

Find the stickers and put them in place. Look at the pictures, then fill in the right double letters from the grid to complete the words.

Example:

book

br__m

ca____ot

pu____y

f____t

dre____

bu____les

oo
ee
ss
rr
pp
bb

Groups of letters

Some words sound the same, but are spelled differently. Look at the words on the roof of the house and write the ones that sound the same in the same window.

sale

hair

hare

pear

pair

sail

Word ladders

Look at the words in these ladders.
Put a check beside the ones you think are spelled correctly.

shoping	shopping
leaves	leeves
swimming	swiming
noyse	noise
calendar	calender
potatoe	potato
samwitch	sandwich

Seasons

Find the stickers and put them in place.

Spring

How many things begin with **r**?

Summer

How many things begin with **s**?

Fall

How many things begin with **b**?

Winter

How many things begin with **c**?

Crossword

Find the stickers and put them in place. Write the names of the musical instruments that are pictured in the crossword. Use the words in the box to help you.

banjo   drum
piano   oboe
guitar   trumpet

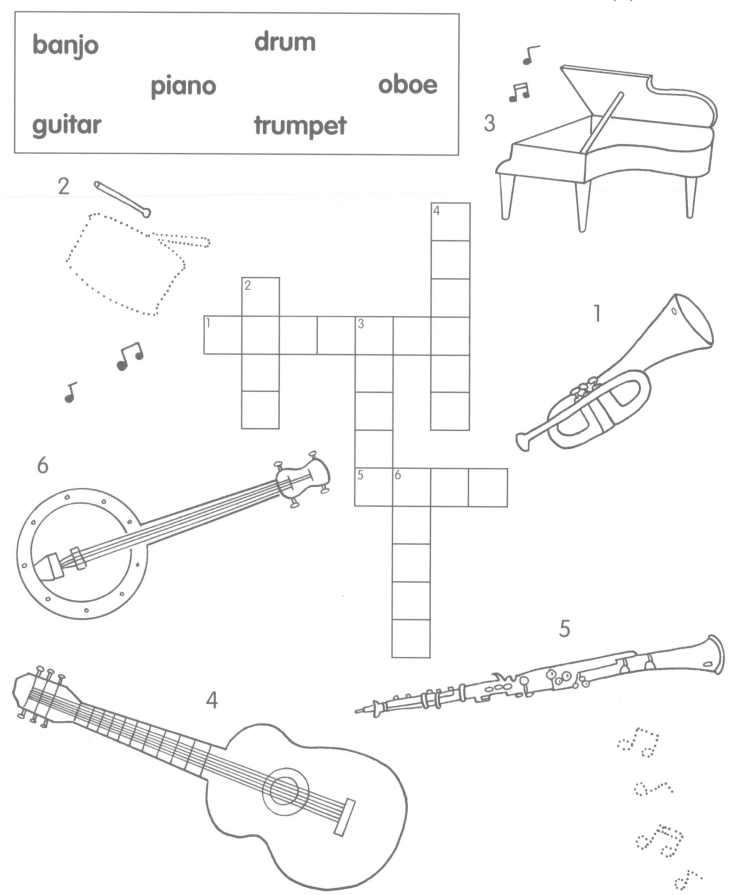

Animals

Find the stickers and put them in place.
Fill in the missing letters to complete the names of these animals.

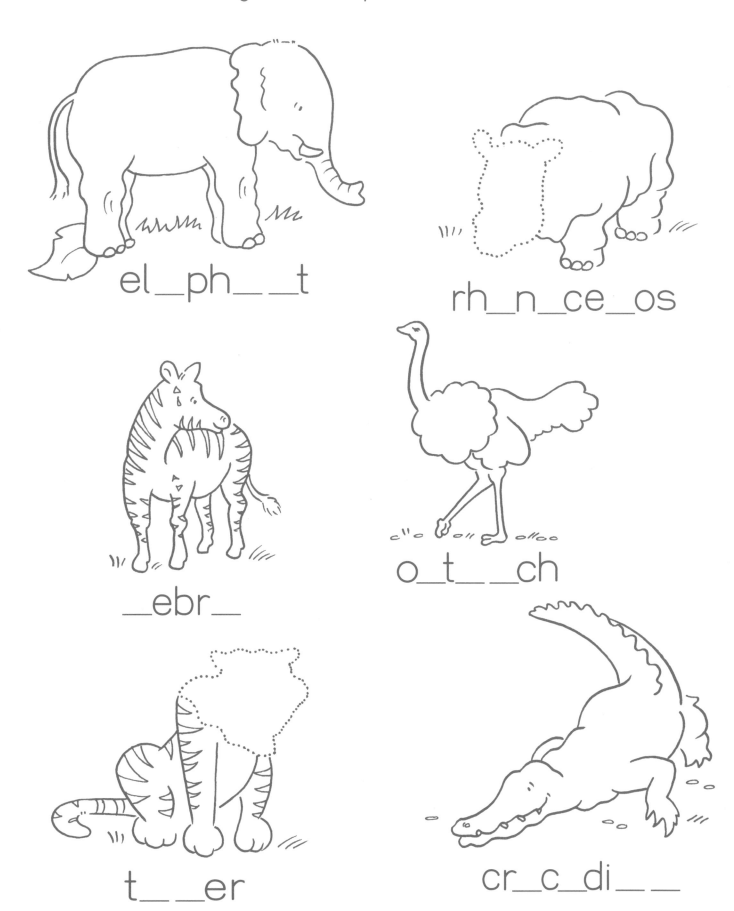

el_ph_ _t

rh_n_ce_os

ebr

o_t_ _ch

t_ _er

cr_ _c_di_ _

Wordsearch

Find the stickers and put them in place. Find these fruits in the wordsearch grid. You will find them by reading across or down. Circle the words as you find them.

```
X  S  R  A  S  O  H  T  M
W  Z  B  P  T  C  D  F  Y
X  T  A  R  R  E  A  X  P
P  I  N  E  A  P  P  L  E
Z  P  A  U  W  I  P  M  A
L  I  N  O  B  C  L  O  R
E  U  A  H  E  X  E  K  E
M  G  I  Y  R  O  D  U  W
O  C  H  G  R  A  P  E  S
N  T  E  O  Y  Y  N  V  A
```

Adding s or es

When you have more than one of something this is called a plural.
Some plurals can be spelled by adding **s**, and some by adding **es**.
Look at the list and change these words into plurals.

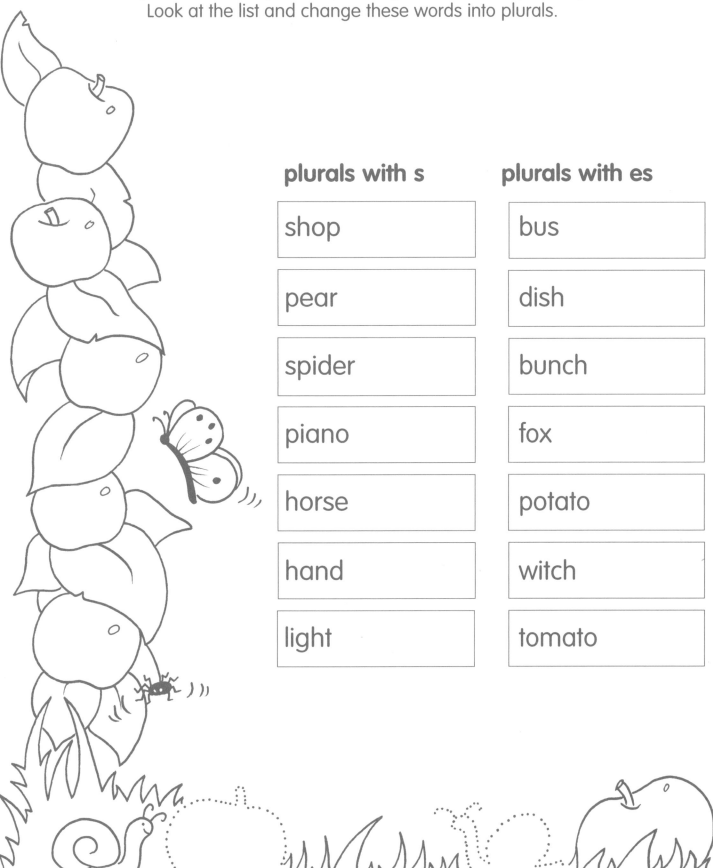

plurals with s

shop

pear

spider

piano

horse

hand

light

plurals with es

bus

dish

bunch

fox

potato

witch

tomato

Hidden words

The words on the cups have a word hidden in them.
Draw a line under the word. Look at the example on the first cup.

done
gone
bones
phone

wanted
elephants
plants
chant

wander
sandal
candle
grandpa

Fruit

Find the stickers and put them in place. Fill in the missing letters to spell
the names of the fruit.

apple

pecch

cherries

ba_ _n_

_ra_es

me_on

o_ _nge

_e_r

Letters s or z

In some words the letter **s** sounds like **z**. Look at the words in the big kite.
Write the words that sound like **s** in one of the smaller kites and the words
that sound like **z** in the other.

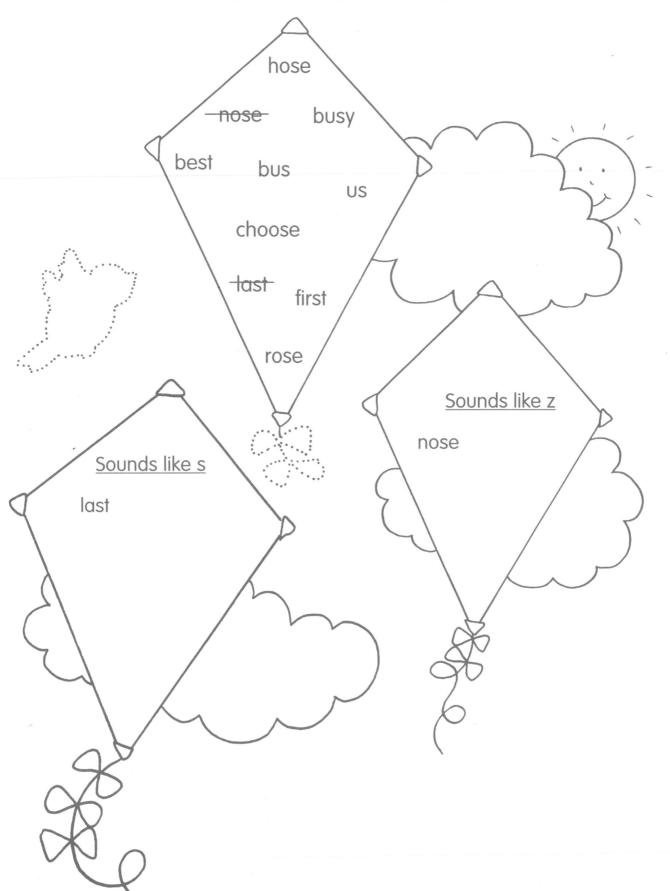

hose

~~nose~~   busy

best   bus

us

choose

~~last~~   first

rose

Sounds like s

last

Sounds like z

nose